Popeye in Belgrade

JAMES SUTHERLAND-SMITH was born in Aberdeen in 1948 and works for the British Council in Belgrade. His work as a Peacekeeping Manager has enabled him to experience first-hand the difficult era of transition in the Balkans particularly through his close contact and work with the armed forces of Serbia and Montenegro. His previous poetry collections include *A Singer from Sabiya* (1979), *Naming of the Arrow* (1980), *At the Skin Resort* (1999) and, with Carcanet, *In the Country of Birds* (2003). James Sutherland-Smith and his wife Viera are the principal translators of Slovak poetry into English, with a number of collections of individual poets and three major anthologies published in Britain, America, Canada and Slovakia.

T0159865

Also by James Sutherland-Smith from Carcanet Press

In the Country of Birds

JAMES SUTHERLAND-SMITH

Popeye in Belgrade

CARCANET

First published in Great Britain in 2008 by
Carcanet Press Limited
Alliance House
Cross Street
Manchester M2 7AQ

A CIP catalogue record for this book is available from the British Library
ISBN 978 1 85754 969 0

The publisher acknowledges financial assistance from Arts Council England

Typeset in Bembo by XL Publishing Services, Tiverton
Printed and bound in England by SRP Ltd, Exeter

Contents

Acknowledgements

'To an Eleven-Year-Old Boy Unable to Speak More Than Two Words' appeared in *A Poetry Quintet* published by Victor Gollancz in 1976.

'Killing a Sheep' was broadcast in *The Country of Rumour* in the BBC Radio 3 series 'The Living Poet' in 1985.

'A Slovak Christmas Tree' appeared in the anthology *Light Unlocked* published by Enitharmon Press in 2005.

Poems in this collection have also appeared in the following magazines, both electronic and print: *Acumen*, *Berkeley Cooperative*, *Caesura*, *Fine Madness*, *Kansas Quarterly*, *Kayak*, *Magma*, *Negative Capability*, *The North*, *Omens*, *Piedmont Literary Review*, *PN Review*, *Poetry Review*, *Qualm*, *Serbian Literary Magazine*, *Signals*, *Stand*, *STIG*, *West Branch*, *The Windless Orchard*.

The Seventies

I started out in Balham in a flat
Where there was a mulberry in the downstairs garden.
The woman I loved would sit on the steps outside
Wearing a dress the colour of its fruit.

Across the road was accommodation
For the clients of the Salvation Army.
We made love with the curtains and windows open
Believing our cries would sound like damnation.

I worked my way north through Battersea,
Fulham, Regent's Park, Camden Lock to Parliament Hill.
I polished my manners and pursued the beautiful
And the rude and not so beautiful pursued me

Although once a lovely tenor voice,
Way above my head as I lay sunbathing
Below the glass pavilions at Kew,
Suggested we divert ourselves at his place

Promising 'Stairway to Heaven' or sweeter themes
Back towards the heart of things on the District Line.
I took his cigarette and inhaled the smoke,
The museum of rare pollens, the stink of the Thames.

Popeye in Belgrade

What if Popeye fails to arrive in the nick of time?
Would Bluto know how to fool around with Olive Oyl?

'C'mon do yuh woist!' she ululates then sighs
As Bluto drums his fists on the ground, 'That's yuh woist?'

Not that Popeye packs all that much of a punch.
Not a single amorous peck in seventy years

Belying the squeaks and wails of baby Swee'pea
Undulating like a rapid snail from frame to frame.

'Is smoking that pipe all yuh can do?' Olive never said that.
Popeye never bubbled through his lips an answer in Serbian,

Never the sort to loll butt naked next to the Sava
Shielding his private parts from the rigours of the sun

Though Bluto might be a suitable size and shape
And possessing the right amount of facial hair.

Unfulfilled desires wriggle over the horizon
Where my wife is smuggling spinach into the EU.

'Serbian spinach is unique,' were her parting words.
I tilt a dram of a liquor made from quince,

Popular but not always available
As the clouds take the shape of rubbery limbs

Shimmying in slow motion. I, too, have danced like that
Earning true devotion for once in my life

And the soubriquet, 'Snake Hips', from a lady,
Hungarian, of uncertain hopes and years

Plumper than Olive Oyl and whose eyes were not black beads.
In passing she patted my tail gently whispering

'Barking bitches don't bite especially
When they take out their teeth before they sleep.'

Off-Duty in Belgrade

With a nod to John Lennon

NATO came and made such neat holes
In the buildings on Kneza Miloša;
The Ministry of Defence, a children's hospital,
The Military HQ, quite geometrical
Taking out almost only what was necessary.

From the rattletrap No. 40 bus
Packed to irritation and breathlessness,
I look at them as though at abstract art.
By the crossroads where I get off I turn
To gaze at another grand illusion,

The largest basilica almost ever, Saint Sava,
A hemisphere whose bare interior
Are concrete pillars and the smell of dust.
Its motes make the light gaudy over tourists
And the few icons set in a single niche.

Belgrade, the white city. I prefer to pun;
Belli gradus, steps down to howitzers
High above where Danube and Sava join.
War compels new, painful starts though I'm old here
Among proud young Serbs, jet-haired, hand in hand.

At night brow-beaten ladies cluster
In cafés beside a taxi rank.
They check their make-up and bombed out charms
So what they offer will pass muster
When their cellphones chime calling them to arms.

I walk through rain and light with a brand new skill
Proud in the middle of my sixth decade
That I can roll a cigarette and spill nothing,
Though not so proud of my employer who tried to find
How many holes it took to kill Belgrade.

After a Funeral

As predicted the clumps of Golden Rain
In the embassy staff gardens have displayed
A blossom of barley sugar yellow,
Papery like the wrappers from the sweets
An aunt would buy us when we behaved.

On the damp lawns lungwort and primrose
Are not themselves, but minor prophecies.
Below a concrete balustrade a quince tree
Hunches like an extra in a movie
Set in medieval or fantastic times.

It plays a churl, all sackcloth and stringy hair,
As the clouds change colour and tumble in
From the coasts and snowy peaks of Illyria
Bringing floods in three daft days of downpour.
And fifty miles due south there's a tremor,

Which tears a strip from the corners of town halls,
Inflicts a hairline fracture down main streets,
And shudders through your fragile bones and cells
So you take to bed, blood pressure falling,
Requesting tea and absolute quiet.

The chimera's coffin has been interred
Under a linden tree as though a saint had died.
Everywhere, in time, it is predicted
His white head of hair will poke through weeds
Unremarkable as a common thistle.

Incident in Novi Sad

I could not sleep.
My little wife snored
In time to puffs of wind
Which rippled in the drapes
So it seemed that mice ran up and down.

I could not sleep
Like many others
After the bombs had stopped.
I pulled my tracksuit on
And took to the starlit streets.

The power lines were down.
No gas, so no traffic.
I walked to the Danube,
A large roly-poly man
Who loves bad jokes, erotica,

The English language
More than the Yanks or Brits.
The jets had come and gone.
That sound like a million
Fingernails across a windowpane

Had stopped. The air smelt sweet.
The bombs had dropped elsewhere.
A nightingale sang.
Truly, just then it sang.
I rolled the word 'dulcet' round my tongue.

I reached the river
And saw the water flicker
Whitely on the stanchions
Of a broken bridge.
I thought of English rhetoric

Demolishing our bridges
And TV masts; Swift,
Johnson, Burke, Adams,
Jefferson, Hamilton become
Smart bombs. By then the nightingale

Had stopped and I heard
The couples' voices
Whimpering in the grass
Along the river side.
Starlight gave their limbs and faces

A pure transparency.
I'm a roly-poly man
Who loves erotica,
But more than a glance
On that occasion would have been,

I think, a little more
Than just intrusive.
I walked back to where I live.
My little wife had
Not stopped snoring. I did not wake her.

A Dream in Serbia

The bride and bridegroom were naked before the priest whose black beard grew to his knees. Like beams of light, cotton gauze floated down and dressed the bride while she patiently stood until she shone.

The bridegroom's suit flowed up his legs from the floor of the church. On his back we could see the inscription in brass lettering, which had been inlaid on the limestone slabs, 'He gave his life.'

The eyes of the icons set in the walls above the congregation glittered in cobalt and vermilion. Their hands lifted jerkily in despair towards the roof of the basilica.

The bride and bridegroom were blessed and drifted outside slightly above the floor of the church as though they were balloons while a brass band serenaded them with a sound like men who had not drunk anything for years.

The wedding procession passed through a village across a stream where fresh leaves, not water, rushed furiously under the bridge. I followed because I had been a witness at the wedding.

I noticed that I had grown the breasts of a teenage girl. The bride and bridegroom brought the village barber to me. He bled me in the traditional way saying it would cure my condition, though whether his treatment was for having the breasts of a girl or for being distressed by them I could not say.

Drops of my blood splashed into a cracked enamel bowl and stained the barber's long grey beard.

Dubrovnik

What intelligence comes from the sea?
The tourists waddle off their cruiser,
Their flip-flops sticking and unsticking
From the soles of their feet.

In the alleys swifts scream, tilt and fade
Above light commerce. Their lines of flight
Are rubbed out against the dusk
As soon as they are made.

A breeze stirs bunting for the Pope,
A tittering white and yellow.
He and his court will come from the sea
In a growl of power boats.

We walk through the hustle of Dubrovnik
To the seaward side of the city
To a café on the cliff where the wine
Is pricey and acidic.

There we gaze down at the shocks
Of waves against endurance
While around us skinny cats filch crabs
From crevices in the rocks.

A Night of Demons

It takes the last of the day's brightness with it,
A red fritillary sideslipping
A spider's trapthread cantilevered between leaf and leaf towards

Dusk. So lacewing, waxwing, a dither of something
Ramshackle, entirely feelers and long, loose legs,
A waltz of bronze eyelashes from carpet to skirting board,
The mosquito's impression of a high speed dentist's drill

All before moths begin to cover the glass of the cabin door.
The largest is the colour of cut wood,
The smallest a corner of a dirty bandage.
In between flutter slivers of stone or leaves deprived of light.

Outside is the growl of a stream over rock,
Energies that knot and tangle to the Black Sea.
Later I may shine my torch on water and glimpse
The tremor of a trout's fin, the spasm of a crayfish tail.

Goatsucker, frog, a sidling in the grass;
On the porch I brush away cobwebs from my face
Not an architecture, but a stickiness of scraps of cloth.
Then the unlikely angel; a bat, its toppling flight,
Catching insects as if from the crests of fast-moving ghosts of waves.

The Clouds of Van Oort

A fritillary; Shepherd's, Heath or Pearl Bordered,
Fastens its wings up for the night to hide
Its varieties of orange and burnt gold
And display a more cautious pattern,
Veined segments of pale brown and green.

So, except for its black tongue, which unfurls
And zips up again as its body trembles,
It could be a piece of bark or drying leaf
Hanging from the zodiac of canework
I've put up on the cabin's whitewashed brick.

It'll be safe from the skittering bat,
Too much of a mouthful for the swallows to eat,
Flickers of blue and white gathering
On the power line stretching to the valley's turn
Under clouds with the bouffant shape and sheen

Of the brittle perms of dowagers
Until they thin to the wisps of extreme old age
And a breeze touches my neck dryly
Like a great uncle or great aunt unsure
If I could be someone they might have met before.

Are the swallows preparing to depart?
I crave that speck of mineral which imparts
To them a vision of the earth's magnetic field.
Do they perceive lines of force like rays of light?
For their young two years on the wing before they mate.

Tonight I'll crane my neck to watch the galaxy
Unfasten brilliance like a butterfly
As the skies clear of both youth and age
And shooting stars curve down in a southern arc
Seemingly purposeful as a swallow flock.

Once more I'll wonder if a random thought
Can move as far and fast as a comet
Brushing by the earth on its huge elliptic
Round the sun, then back to cold space and on out,
Longer than mankind, to the Clouds of Van Oort.

Red Poet

i.m. Ján Ondruš (1932–2001)

I incinerated my first poems.
A fine blaze they made, the colour of yolk.
I ensured not a syllable was left,
Powdering the ash and mixing it with piss.
I wasn't able to grow a beard then.
So I daubed on a false moustache
From the paste I'd made. I stripped off
And covered myself with secret signs,
Danced uttering an unknown language
Its meaning secret even to me.

The first book I allowed I called *Black Egg*,
A magical phrase taken from Sanskrit.
The universe is an egg.
There are many universes,
In frogspawn, in the banks of the Nile,
In a lark's nest speckled with dark suns.
You can drop an egg from a high window.
It won't break when full of language.
There are stones exactly like eggs.
If a man held a stone his whole life long
It wouldn't break either, but grow warm.
It would hatch into a poem, a stone bird.

If you take a needle and pierce and blow
What comes from the egg is a kind of light
Sometimes veined or streaked with red.
This means that something grew inside.
You can't eat it. The red is poetry.
You can't eat a poem. It tastes bad.
We are streaks of red inside the universe.
What we know as light drools through windows.

After my first book I had enough to live
In the house of the executioner.
There was work in a library;
So many books without a hint of red.
I couldn't manage to burn them all.
Occasionally I'd snaffle volumes
On birds or architecture or stones
And fill my stove. I'd go outside
And try to read the wing beat or arch
Or avalanche of smoke. No meaning there.
I am a universe, egg-like.
I sit in the centre of my bed
My legs tucked up to my chin,
My arms folded round my knees.
If I had a razor I'd shave my skull.
My hands are the problem. They hold secrets.
Light from another universe
Bends and slithers into their palms.

Where does the light go? Into my blood?
No. It goes out of the back of my hands.
Sometimes I pull at the skin there.
It is still elastic. When it begins
To sag and wrinkle that is entropy
And my hands will be black holes
Absorbing light and gravity and time.

Until then hunters of secrets come
And stick needles into me.
They try to suck out my light, my red streaks.
I don't resist. I watch them carefully.
Nothing escapes from me. Not a sound.
I hold the great secret of poetry.
Why am I silent? Why don't I speak?
It wouldn't be a secret then, would it?

The Little Fiddler

Ornamentation

We have adorned a white wall with scars,
Yours a child's fiddle
The varnish chipped, not a secret of the Cremonese,
The strings floppy, the pegs loose.
But there it is, a lesion of sycamore and spruce
Ornamental on a white wall
Above a pot of philodendron out of control.
Seven years you toiled like a lost princess
And swore off all childish games and squabbles.
In your heart there's no silliness
Only the passacaglia of duty correct and formal.
Never call the fiddle an airy instrument
Though you might take its compass
Beyond Biber's high A squeal.
Call a scar an ornament
With its Archimedean scroll
Its proportions from Pythagoras.
You now hate all things mathematical
And dust down your fiddle
The thing itself scratched and tuneless
Containing silence, all childhood's loss.

At Play

To step out into a morning sun
Untrammelled by cloud
Before science was known to you.
So it is there like a flower
Or a god you can't look in the eye
Because of what he might do to you.

Your midmorning shadow,
Neither taller nor shorter than the real you,
Bulges because of the fiddle case
Swinging slightly by your side.

It's Saturday and you could be playing
One of a hundred simple games.

But you'll play music and scrape and scrape
Until a line of melody
Or arpeggio or phrase will come out true.
The sweaty god with pomade in his hair
Will beam at you, a once blond son
Of a people giving awards for culture.

A Game

One Saturday morning there was a single uncovered window.
There was a dog running out front
And there was an enormous tension
As if a string quartet were tuning up
On a diving board high above an empty swimming pool.
For this was the dream you'd had.

The sun had come up raising a whole foot in deliberation.
Closing your eyes you stepped out
Choosing a different foot for each step
As if you were a caterpillar
Always another foot, another for the stair, another for the invisible
Watering can placed in your path,

The basket, the stone, the burdock plant reaching to your shoulder.
You paused knowing where you were
Just inside the gate, fiddle case in hand
While something joyous and panting ran past
On the pavement that unseen loop of asphalt stretching to the lesson,
With tussocks of grass to be stepped over.

He blindfolded you that day so you could feel the intervals
Rather than watch your fingers,
His fingers resting on the nape of your neck.
Do you remember correctly?
They slid ever so gently over your T-shirt and came to rest
Where your spine joins your buttocks.

From then on you walked to music lessons, fiddle case in hand,
                                        eyes wide open.

Invitation to a Pig-Killing

Your hair falling from an exact parting
In the centre of your head,
Wavy, thick, each hair a slightly different shade,
Shoulder length, shapely, symmetrical
The outline of a violin without fret board.
The wind tried to blow a tune into your hair.
Discipline, years of practice kept it in order.
I shall say moderato.

You'd been sent forth from the house
Fiddle case in hand.
Your parents wished to show you off.
You would play while sausage skins were stuffed.
You would play while a haunch turned on a spit
And vodka was lavished even on you.
C'mon you're seventeen...
And cousin Miro would wipe his fingers clean
He'd've read somewhere
                    We have to touch to know.

For far too long you'd crook a knuckle
Before knocking on that particular door.
There'd be a salvo of popping corks.
Auntie would dispense tripe soup with a ladle.
Steam would whistle through the cookhouse keyhole.
You'd raise and tune your lovely fiddle
Resting on that space between neck and lovely breast.

A World of Music

The music man with his cap on the ground
And his toothless carnivorous stare
Makes the world succulent with his repertoire
Though his is not the only sound.

There's a horrible scraping from the main street,
A dawdle of Bach and Mendelssohn from the square.
For it's spring and the beggars come out from their lair
To display their stumps and misshapen feet

For money, some kneeling in postures of abasement
Making no sound whatever though they pucker their lips
And their hands twitch right down to their fingertips
As if they played an invisible instrument.

You walk between them fiddle case in hand
Knowing that it only takes one false note
For you to tumble down the scale and share their fate.
From harmony to cacophony: you've found

It needs a semi-tonal, a micro-tonal slip.
So you walk between disaster and disaster,
The dread of error, like your music master,
Lathering you about the head with his cap.

Fiddler with Card Players

Blind drunk they have faces
You do not care to touch. You stop down faces

With your naked fingertips. You hold your face
At least an arm's length from their faces

And your face is always vertically
Adjusted on your tears not their lopsided grins

Thrown into your wound, your distaste,
You stop down, you carry like a pinch of salt.

Look, they say, pour your face into our wounds
Smile at us with a pinch of salt.

Let us take your face to our lips,
Let us slurp up its saltiness.

And they turn away overtrump face with face,
Slap face face down on face.

You play a gale through your two faces
Opened against each other.

You release your face from its chains,
Grind your face against your face,

Lock your face with the key of the fiddle case
Which belongs to your other face.

Your face arises, vanishes and you lower
Your bow and become a face among faces.

A Score Settled

The fiddler goes to buy buttons.
She wishes someone would buy her gold earrings.

She goes up the street and isn't cold for once.
She won't pause for old men's congratulations
Or for children who shout, I saw you on TV!

She doesn't hobble under the weight of fame.
She doesn't hop, step and jump in a children's game.

She'll set light to that score
She practised for seven years or more

And from the frail paperyness that she gets
She'll cut out dry, blue silhouettes

Of the flower of her looks tipped up to my gaze,
The star she ran under a fingernail,

The migraines she tried to blink out over days,
Until the nights came and bound her eyes in knots from the
                                                    moon's rays.

Giant Burdock

A giant burdock by our cabin in the woods:
It is depression's spiky flower
So tall it bends over you
Making you so tiny, a Thumbelina
Lost without mouse or frog or bird to rescue her.

We drive away and come to rest outside our house
Beneath our apricot tree.
You nothing lack, you nothing wish
Is what you keep telling me.
Inside our daughter listens to Tartini,

The Devil's Sonata unaccompanied
Though you don't appear to hear it
Or conversation from next door,
Sparrow squabble, the minute
Sounds of traffic in the Sunday streets.

You don't stop me when I disentangle from your hair
A burdock seed caught there by chance.
Inside the burr is mottled turquoise,
A bead for a necklace of faience,
At which you do not even glance.

As I crush it to a powder that won't take root
Our daughter shuts her window against the heat
And the Devil's virtuosity grows quiet.
The neighbours murmur on while at our feet
A Red Admiral feasts on rotting apricot.

A Dead Mouse

We found it beside the felled walnut tree
Thumbjoint-sized, thimble neat,
Paws raised in minute supplication,
Bark-coloured except for the yellow fleck of its anus
That you noticed, which I had to put glasses on to see.

We thought it dead from cold or the noise of the chainsaw
So placed the mouse on a walnut leaf
Whose middle segment drooped like a Florida
Torn off from America.
Branches lopped, the tree lay ready to be made good money.

I picture you mouse-nervously
Lifting a violin with walnut veneer
Its lavish burnt-honey grain between your chin and breasts,
Its harmonics higher than a mouse's cry
Pitched against winter coming on, against becoming money.

Reaction

As if fears could be shed
Like leaves from the unwatered plant
Gaunt in its pot in the corner,

As if there could be instead
Of your custom of hearing aslant
Everything I say, a grand gesture

Which changes you from the key of dread
To happiness. No, only adjustment
As if to the loss of empire

My generation had drummed into its head,
All truth to follow a dissent
From such glory and the rapture

Of what overflowed from our island bed
Where we now lie completely silent.
Above us the ceiling has discoloured

Where the banging rain has seeped and spread
From the skylight, the shape of a continent
Whose heart was glass and the glitter

As if the god, Eros, had passed overhead;
A moment's faith, then diminishment
Into other truths, the absence of desire.

Inspiration

The lovely curve of the neck of the fiddle
The scroll of hair you let fall:

Resist that. Think of someone gentle
Sounding herself, a trill

Momentary yet not trivial
A language which is musical

Which is more than you thought to say
Which is what I wish to take away

Your harmonics, your quarter tones
The sound of water over stones.

The First Snow of Christmas

Snow makes a slight sound like a nurse's sleeve
And clings to the branches of the pine
Producing shapes like plaster casts
Round classical statues or broken limbs;
This one a satyr shiftingly obscene,
That one an arm set at right angles.

Beneath our windows a family searches
For a lost puppy or a kitten.
They shine thin torch beams on the snow
And I'm reminded of sunlight
Wavering across the seabed in patches
Until a shadow falls across the glitter.

It's not a cloud across the moon but the gypsy
We sent packing earlier today.
I'd given him money three days before,
Complimented the ink-blue suit
He'd received at the pastor's door.
He was bald, single-toothed and skinny,

An unshaven Nosferatu though not ashen
And afraid of light, but mahogany.
In one hand he carried a violin.
His other gripped my own, his thumbnail
Digging to leave a wedge-shaped flaw
That still aches as the winter cold sets in.

I rub it as he pauses in the snow
And takes his violin from its case
To play a scratchy, hardwood music.
He salutes our windows then hides his face
As the torches are clicked off one by one
And a rough northerly begins to blow.

A Rite of Spring

My mother-in-law foretold a clear, raw night.
Frost would spoil blossom of scrupulous white
Except for reddening where petals joined their stem.
To pluck flowers might have pricked a tree, caused harm.

Their scent was delicate, too sweet almost
And there was bitterness, a sorrow that would last.
I touched the trunk of an apricot, its fissures
Were like those of trees grown for lifetimes, not years.

I was dismissed after duty as a porter.
The barbecue became a sacred brazier.
Charcoal and kindling were composed on it.
My mother-in-law brought wood blanched from rot.

My wife, her mother, my daughter were to smoke
The apricot trees. Resigned, stubborn and ironic,
Woman, crone and maiden wrapped in hoods
Were to flap or conjure smoke over flower heads.

As night fell I watched the foolish or the wise
Feed wood on to the lucid heat beneath the trees
And become mysterious, vanishing from sight
As the blade of moon and the stars were blotted out.

At sunrise the garden glinted like scratched tin
Though round the trees were circles of moist green.
In late July branches of the apricots
Split and fell from the weight of perfect fruit.

Blewits

I have lost all sense of proportion.
I can't measure what is more intense,
The sky's blue after rain after weeks of drought
Or your eyes' forget-me-not after months of pain.

On your grandparents' tomb we sit and lightly knock.
There just might be somebody at home.
A hollow sound is what we hear, for the earth
Has shrivelled and rain has hardly wet the ground.

Below us a breeze thrums the raggle-taggle shingles
On the sides of an empty house. A guard dog booms
As though it barked from the bottom of a well
And two hunters show from an orchard's dark.

Under leaf mould in the wood we have found blewits
Beside yellow mushrooms too gorgeous to be good.
The blewitts we set out upon your family stone
Are rayed beneath, firm to the touch, violet.

The hunters stop to talk, the man carrying
A rifle with an ornamental stock,
The girl in felt boots and army fatigues.
A dead rabbit twirls head down from her belt.

They both kneel, sniff, declare our mushrooms edible.
The rabbit jiggles on her belt as the girl moves off.
They will skin it, hang it for a day, then stew it.
I wonder how rabbit tastes prepared with blewits.

Comfrey

They are the Victorian era.
Their leaves are heavy overskirts,
Their purple flowers the sober colour of a ribbon

A Florence Nightingale might tie her hair with
As she attends the bruises, cuts
That comfrey salves. Cherry, plum and peaches ripen

And the wild rose is more glamorous
But all summer long the bee alights
On comfrey. A deep sweetness is taken from its dark green

Which broadens and grows hairier
As all else dries, seeds and rots
Until it, too, lolls on earth, the tongue of a sleeping dragon.

Making Hay

The skill deserves a book to itself
As intricate as Ovid's Art of Love.

I once jarred the tip of a scythe against a stone
And a doctor tapped fluid from my elbow for a month.

A good steady sway and twist of your hips
Is needed to keep the blade parallel to the earth,

A motion not completely semi-circular
But in a sizeable arc and you will learn

That meadowgrass, cow parsley, fireweed, clover topple
In neat swathes all the more easily to be forked

Round a stook's frame, a wooden A tacked together
From loose two-by-two left spare from other work.

Make hay though your hands blister, forearms and shoulders ache.
Who knows when there'll be a change in the weather?

Afterwards wipe your scythe down and lean it against a wall.
The iron blade curves like a giant raven's feather.

Watching the Weather

This is not the first line I was advised to write,
That being supposedly rather more snappy.
I'll get to it by and by though you won't notice.
The weather is so changeable I've veered from the tight,
Controlled lyric to something altogether looser.
At the moment I'm in the porch watching smoke rise
From the chimney of a kitchen in an outhouse
Built by my wife's grandfather, an atheist,
Who in the war fed the partisans and hid
Caches of weapons no one has found to this day.
It's said he could feel approaching weather in his bones,
Which is all my wife has left in her of country lore.
Her head aches long before I can sense a storm.
I'm watching smoke rise despite the steady rain
And the biggest clap of thunder I've ever heard
In Slovakia after lightning came so close
I'd stake my life the air sizzled and smelt of sulphur.
Rain has made the trees so definite in detail;
Willow, sycamore, hornbeam, lime are green and precise.
My mother-in-law and I are in shelter;
Hoe, rake and scythe abandoned. We've discussed the absence
Of fruit this year, no apples, some pears, some plums
Though the trees have a red spot of blight on each leaf.
I know enough to say in Slovak that the trees
Should be pruned back and sprayed, but I've no idea
How to go about it. There are more walnuts
Than last year, still too green to be picked, and the rain means
There'll be mushrooms by the middle of next week;
The oak, the butter, the parasol, the redhead,
Champignon, which is best fried in olive oil.
The talk turns from food to death as it always does.
So my mind wanders off and I recall a girl
Before my wife from the flat plains round the Vah
At quite the other end of Slovakia.
Her father was a meteorologist
Whose hobbies were tennis and sharpening knives,
A skill his daughter shared. Once I watched her strop

A kitchen knife on leather and then she held
The new edge to my throat and whispered, 'Take care, honey,'
Before she sliced away my belt leaving a slit
All the way down my trouser leg to my knee.
When she was a child, seven or eight years old,
During what was called after 1968
The Era of Consolidation, a graveyard
Was dug up in her town by the Party and its chapel
Turned into offices. She claimed that she and others
Played football with a skull, used thigh bones as goalposts
Stuck in the newly excavated and flattened earth.
Now the graveyard is a green and pleasant place
With courts marked out for volleyball and tennis
Though it's untended round the edge where I once watched her
Stand in grass up to her hips as rain poured down.
I went to her and felt something round beneath my foot.

Here the rain has stopped and thunder passed to Hungary.
What has that girl's father got to do with my wife's grandfather?
Nothing. They could not have known each other.
And weather is so local: here it has rained,
But in the next valley it could be bone dry.
Rain has not fallen all over Slovakia.
We measure what has happened and feel what is to come.
Today the weather comes from Poland, tomorrow
The temperature could be eighty-one degrees.
I miss my wife, her fear of storms and human violence.
Her name is Viera, no not Vera, English reader,
Viera and that line you told me to put first…

In a Slovak Garden

I dig below the cabbages
And above the strawberry patch.
The spade sinks into loam not clay
And I turn it over, break it
And pick out grass and weeds.

Your father tells me
'Don't break the earth.
The winter frosts do that.'
I try it his way for a row,
But the earth looks incomplete.
Once more I turn loam over, break it up.

The widow from next door tells me,
'Don't break the earth.
The winter frosts do that.'
And from the other side
Doričková, who sang folksongs
At our wedding, choruses
'Don't break the earth. Don't break the earth.'

I understand. I understand,
But I try to tell them all
That we do not have hard frosts
In England, that my digging
Is from the habits of my youth.

I try to dig the way I'm told,
But it's worse than learning Slovak.
My spade turns a clod of sound.
A tongue of iron hesitates
And trembles over it as if
To separate consonant from
Consonant, sense from sense.

I think of winter frost
As I dig on so very slowly now,
Not in English, not in Slovak.

Spades and Roses

So much unexpected emotion spent on cleaning our spades,
Scraped clean of soil, hosed and hosed, dried with a rag
Then propped upright or laid prone against the wall
So burnished the setting sun glitters on their blades.
Some of us lie prone on the grass and smoke.

Between each headstone there's now a neat and weeded interval.
Broken vodka bottles, plastic bags, porno mags,
Barbed wire, planks, a mouldering carrycot
Were cast into a skip or burnt if dry and flammable.
All of us cast top clothes aside, worked quickly, hardly spoke

Though now we decide if the place should be left unadorned,
The graffiti being rubbed off or whitewashed over.
Just pebbles have been placed on the headstones of those
Who were ancestors of some of our best friends.
Neither the best nor worst of us seems willing to go.

The synagogue in the town was used to store toilet seats.
One of us suggests planting a few roses.
Another retorts that planting roses in this place
Would be barbaric. Roses, the first repeats,
Roses left almost to themselves will grow and grow.

A weak solution of detergent to keep off greenfly,
Fertiliser, mulching twice a year, when required dead-heading.
What kind of a spade could we use to plant roses?
One with a pointed blade that can cut through clay
Stony ground, caskets of oak and pain, the skull of a maid

Taken before her time, but at last laid peacefully to rest.
The other spade has a straight edge to trim the borders
Of the curving paths which point a dutiful visit
To a far gate and a leave-taking. Which is best?
A spade is a spade is a spade is a spade, is a spade.

A Slovak Christmas Tree

Above the altar floats the Christ Child;
Rosy, plump, baroque he floats free
From the round breasts of the Virgin Mary
Who is all, as they claim here, 'blood and milk'.
He floats in shimmering blue and gold
Beneath the branches of a gaunt tree.

Outside the church we wrap our natures
Against the cold wind and the snow.
Unleaved, linden, ash and beech show
The crookedness the Christ Child endures
From us; bare branches snow-blurred
That the cold wind creaks to and fro.

The Christ Child will burst his rosy bud
To the everlasting green of leaves,
But he'll be fruit for our unbelief
On a gaunt tree whose wood stains red
As each year our sins bud, leaf and shed
While we claim, disclaim, proclaim belief.

Curlew

Grandpa, the regimental quartermaster,
in retirement officer commanding
deployments of cabbages and carrot,
skirmishers of spring onion
beyond ramparts of earth flung up for potatoes,
had little time for flowers,

although parade ground ranks of antirrhinum
edged the lawn with shakos of crimson
while Piers and I doubled widdershins
round the house pursued by a small
black undisciplined sheepdog and our first sister
barely three years old, too young

to know that brothers find little girls a pest
and too young to follow us to the field
where the white dragon lay, an elm trunk
with horns, its bark fallen away
therefore smooth to straddle and never breathing fire.
We thought we heard a curlew.

Who said it was a curlew? Grandpa perhaps,
his ear once alert for grouse or pheasant
or popping of a capercailzie,
after my over-excited
'a ghost crying then blowing bubbles through water!'
remembering the curlew

between 1915 and 1919
on the Prussian marshes beside which he'd dig
beets and potatoes for a farmer
employing prisoners-of-war.
But it seemed our sister, Sarah, had been calling
for us to play hide-and-seek.

Not that I would have obliged her afterwards
except for a look of disappointment
from Grandpa or a clip round the ear
from Father as September came
and I was uniformed, tuckboxed then sent to school
where I cried myself to sleep.

One night after being mocked out of my tears
I heard a curlew call on the common.
'Smith Two is barmy,' whispered Sawyer,
'It's the nine o'clock from London,
Castle Class, from the tremble in the whistle tone.'
Oh curlew, little sister.

Running

from Cuckoo Pen past Aycote farm and the hedge
behind which we'd play with the Wilkins boys,
Stephen, twelve, swift runner at secondary modern
in Cirencester – 'Do you do Latin?' 'Mebbe' –
David, seventeen, occasionally
ducking and diving through the copse by their cottage,
on his wide shoulders their little sister
and my brother, once not running rather
hobbling just after circumcision, his bandage
unravelling from under one leg of his short trousers;

so running away from him up the lane
past the conifers beyond, left at the post box
on to a short slope until a signpost,
so left again towards Woodmancote
to the stile and the path across the meadow
leading him and me to Sunday school
with Pauline of the bobbed hair the colour of barley
and Peggy of the pigtails gleaming like liquorice,
who once at the Christmas Party in Spin-the-Plate
laid it flat and called me to forfeit a kiss;

so leap from the stile and go right past the Co-op
and Grandpa Smith's sweatshop, G.B. Smith and Sons,
employing only the old at a rate
'which would not detract from their pensions',
over the railway then under the railway bridge
on to fields towards Trent Lock where young 'un,
our kid, had his first jump wi' Deirdre H——,
turning right on to the towpath by Erewash Canal
and houseboat of Michelle J—— said to have
pubic hair all the way up to her navel;

so sprint to the grammar school along Tamworth Road,
Cluley cycling past as part of me trudged home
shouting 'Plastic surgery!' despite his nose
and chin indicating one of Mr Punch's byblows

not to mention that as time ran by I found
that good manners was all I was required to show
in the final stagger past the fire station
with thirty-eighth my best position
and for fifteen years little exercise at all
until the run from the refinery village,

a left and right to the North African highway
sometimes dodging stones thrown by a boy
at this infidel though not on the coastal track,
only for the seriously athletic
or for long tall Crosbie mooning after goat boys,
killed in Amsterdam by someone he annoyed
and left again out of the Mess in Riyadh
then right and right again on to the main road,
twenty minutes all the way down to the Garden Centre
right again up a sharp slope, then a long canter

past long-distance lorries parked bumper to bumper,
eighty or ninety degrees in the dry evening,
though all right with sips from a flask of water
right again on to the airport perimeter past villas
each wall the same colour of distemper
once a mutawah driving his Chevrolet
across my path gobbing over my T-shirt
after he's wound down his window and bellowed
'If I so catch you so naked so
I will so taken you so to prison so beat you!'

so left out of my front door in fundamentalist
Norfolk, left down the Norwich Road, a right twist,
a left twist, a long incline to just
before the roundabout near Norfolk's highest
point, 287 feet,
and to Peddar's Way, a Roman route
through Iceni country, past the ash trees, right
on to the bridle path back to Swaffham that
the Suevi settled, right into the kitchen
for a glass of water before switching

off the light so I can gaze through the window
at the few winter lamps of Švaby that
Swabian artisans settled, blurred by snow
swirling right and right again until I view
myself rolling in bed, an old disassociation,
dreaming perhaps both sleeper walking and sleeper prone,
yet right and right again to prove it is a dream
for snow shouldn't turn the corner of the block
so precisely and in such slow motion,
each snowflake a six-pointed star, unique

until compacted into snowdrift, ice, meltwater
running through the drains to the Sekčov, turning
left into the Torysa then right into the Tiszva
then left into the Danube, straight on to the Black Sea
to be taken up and shed elsewhere as rain
north of the Caucasus where maybe, mebbe,
our related various tongues were born,
words in common drifting westwards hardly changed
to Aycote farm; stooks of hay, at water ewes,
the apple trees, the Wilkins boys calling 'Cuckoo!'

Screech Owls

Like the noise from a litter of newborn kittens
Or loose hinges on an unlatched gate,
Which the wind swings forth and gravity tugs back,
An unfleshly squealing arises at sunset
By the mustard yellow church in the lindens.

I went to look armed with a screwdriver
And found not human neglect and absence
But four charcoal-faced Socratic screamers
Shifting from claw to claw in the boughs, an eloquence
Of the great themes of nesting, sex and hunger.

That was the second night, but on the first
You went out alone in your light green nightdress
With milk for something abandoned and in pain.
This is the third night and neither foolish tenderness
Nor fake practicality go out. We fear the worst;

A boy with an air rifle, a drunk with a stone
Getting lucky. Yet round here people do not say
Coals to Newcastle, but owls to Athens
As though the birds were part of local speech. So I pray
That what is commonplace is left well-alone
By those sensitive to unlucky omens.

On Not Reading L'Allegro

As is usual on the stopping train from work
I'm reading something canonical, which I've divided
Into ten episodes of one hour's attention;
This week a paperback of Milton's *Selected*
Among the garlic breath and vodka fumes.

I sweat, too, my deodorant ineffective.
With the others I've taken off my jacket
And hung it beneath the luggage rack.
At least we'll arrive looking odourless
And neat at our various destinations.

I envy handsome John's 'sunshine holidays'
Of about four hundred years ago, though then
My grimace and delicacy over body odours
Would have had him rank me with deluded men
Who imagined they were made of glass.

Something has happened outside the train.
It jolts to a halt having hardly started
From a platform too short for all the carriages
As a girl pulls back from the window stifling
A 'Ježiš Mária' with her hand to her mouth.

Others go to the window, look out and wince.
Some do not show the same inclination.
It seems an arm has been trapped in a door.
A severed arm on the track? Should I incline
My gaze away from rhyming couplets?

I do the indecent thing and poke my head out.
A man has wrapped his shattered, but still connected arm,
In his jacket and is being scolded by his wife
For spoiling his new suit, not to mention the harm
To her peace of mind and the groceries he's dropped.

Beyond them in a potato field old women
In pink and lilac pinafores bend over plants
Picking off the beetles they call mandolinky.
They may have stopped for a moment and spared a glance,
But the care of potatoes is more to the point.

The women are multi-coloured mice in the field
Beneath a long cat's paw of cloud, which creeps
Down from the north. What do they do with the beetles?
At night perhaps at this time of year they fall asleep
Counting stripy little buggers not sheep.

In Malaya over fifty years ago
I slammed my brother's little finger in the door
Of a bedroom in a resthouse on Frazer's Hill.
Our father snatched up the cleanest towel and tore it
To bind a finger dangling on a shred of skin.

The finger knitted back though somewhat crooked.
I don't remember our holiday being spoilt.
There were grapefruit trees outside the resthouse.
For years the yellow fruit recalled my fault,
My moment's inattention in closing a door.

Sometimes I wonder if I slammed a door shut
On an aptitude for guitar or piano:
A distant drunken cousin could play jazz,
My youngest sister was praised for her soprano,
In my teens I tried to be a composer

Strumming out my own system of polyphony,
My daughter won a TV singing competition
And blind John Milton sang for his daughter's pleasure.
Sweating, I recall my brother's rapt concentration,
His bandaged hand tilting his first Coca-Cola.

The Silences

Spring, a sniff; summer, a drowse;
Autumn, a long inhalation;
Winter, visible breath, puffed between pursed lips
Attempting figures of eight in the cold air:

We began to take notice
Of when sound was wholly absent
In the desultory hours between school homework
And the TV shows permitted before bedtime.

A ghastly hush when the neighbour
With the Puritan poet's name
Chased his wife down the avenue bawling, 'Trollop!'
His eldest son later convicted of cheque book fraud

In one of those estuary towns
Where land, sea and sky are almost
Horizontal bands of colour, each with murmurs
To be suppressed in case land, sea and sky vibrate.

A ghastly hush following
A girl's screech as if someone
Had dropped a maggot down her neck or grabbed her breasts.
Was ever silence so smug, so neighbourly,

Thinking to itself, 'Serves her right
For being so provoking,'
And preening itself that all such leaps on the clapometer,
As seen on one of the permitted TV shows,

Were part of life as we know it
And were going to know forever
While above us the sky struggled to stir itself,
Clouds shaping a huge fleecy mouth, but saying nothing.

A ghostly hush before
The slow clicking of a bike chain
At approximately five past five, give or take
A standard deviation of three minutes

As the man in the spectacles
With shiny brown frames, a jacket
Not quite matching his brown trousers, brown socks
And unspecked brogues rode by, not forgetting

The slight chink in his saddle bags.
What could they have contained?
What could have the silence, which restored itself
After he'd passed, contained? Menace? Boredom? Saddle polish?

And who's to say whether silence
Arrives in particle or wave form,
Specks of blackness in white stellar noise
Or a sinuous pattern of calligraphy

In a culture where the image
Or human likeness has been banned
And the word as written down centuries before
Must be spoken advisedly and not deviated from?

All this close to the border
With Italy from a young artist
Of no particular talent, who talked loudly
Banging the café table-top between sentences.

I said nothing. Of course,
My point flowed by unnoticed.
I drank my cappuccino trying not to gulp
Or get foam on my moustache as I swallowed each sip.

Cats and Sparrows

Slap bang in the middle of our street the tomcat,
Who regularly chases birds across our lawn,
Is servicing his queen while his best mate
Sits, paws folded beneath his chest, waiting his turn.
Their love-making could not be called amicable,
All growls and hisses, and when they disentangle
The toms slouch off and the queen, still available,
Wriggles under a car on her belly swishing her tail.

Their preoccupation has let the sparrows preen
And sport in puddles. They douse themselves and whirl
Up into our hedge where, hidden in the green,
Their soused fluttering makes each sound like a larger bird.
They have a running dispute, a perpetual brawl
Over who should nest in a crevice in our wall
Beside a cable box just below my windowsill
On which the dominant male perches and calls

Chirrup! Chirrup! between intervals of shitting
And a paranoiac's rage at his reflection
In the outer window panes. Pecking, flitting,
Pecking, flitting, he is not gifted with introspection.
Chirrup! Chirrup! Like a one-issue political
He will convince through repetition and already spoils
My afternoon's close reading, my perusal
Of John Skelton's rhythms and rime royal.

Cat-like, I creep up on him behind the window glass.
He is oblivious, chirping his Delenda est Carthago.
Though chocolate striped he is capped just like a mouse
With a fine grey down. I'm with Gib the cat, who could not say no
And worrowed on Philip Sparrow, even if Lesbia herself fell
Into my arms or Jane Scrope nicely pursed her lips and called
On me for hard rhymes in adequate acquittal
Then pounsed my breast with pretty claws on my refusal.

There's no grief ground I'd have in mind to harrow
For the natural death of Philip Sparrow.
Last year we holidayed where half-starved cats would insinuate
Themselves at dinner for whatever dropped from our plates.
Afterwards before sunset we would stroll
On the corniche between trinket stall and trinket stall.
Overhead a flock of sparrows would bunch or sprawl,
Psychopomps twittering a soul to paradise or hell.

Under a tamarisk we saw a queen cat and her kittens,
Her belly bald, her paps swollen, her noise imperturbable
As her litter sucked. The sparrows faltered at the ocean
Veering their babble inland. The water was so still
We just had to bathe. In that calm our skin was pale,
Almost transparent: we could imagine our muscles
Stretched across our bones, our blood circling
From ventricle through to vein to ventricle.

Our daughter turned her head before she dived, a Roman girl
I could have thought, a Tudor girl. A girl, I thought, a girl.

The Autumn Laundry

You are laying out our winter clothes,
Folding them, replacing them on wooden shelves
Sweet with the smell of soap and jars of pot-pourri,
A different colour, a different essence
For sweaters, shirts, blouses, underwear.
This is not a task I'm allowed to do.
I turn from writing to watch you work
And wonder if I might catch your scent.

Outside is everything you hate;
A brawl, fumes rising as neighbours roast a pig,
Beyond them clouds sharp-edged as splintered timber
Signalling a storm when you will hide your head,
And beyond that perhaps your unlaundered past,
A cousin, boy next door, classmate, the argument
You never wed, who might have blemished you
With those resentments which discolour lives almost
Imperceptibly until the stain is permanent.
You remain serene and cold to this as winter,
Your landscapes immaculate as linen.

Inside is everything you do not hate.
I am your rough weather, your dirty blanket
Laid on the earth between the stalks of maize,
Your blazing row. I have caught your scent.
Outside the pig crackles on the spit while the pure colours,
Browns, reds and lilacs, lift tumblers of sour wine.

Beyond the Glue Factory

We jolt past the bone smell
Where horse head, ox thigh, pig skull
Are rendered down for glue.
Then a three hour wait at a border station
And the bone smell comes in out of the night
Drunk on a day's pay, requesting a light,
An archipelago of piss stains on his overalls,
The stink of the glue vats in the folds of his skin.

Just over the border the bone smell leaves the train.
I watch him fall flat and rise again
As he flounders through the snow to his cottage
Before we accelerate through the hills
Where houses are decked out like Christmas trees.
There is a smell of iron whirling against iron
And new fallen snow beside a foaming river
Has almost the scent of fresh ginger.

We have left the bone smell behind us
And approach the odour of a rebuilt city;
Cigarettes, coffee, walnut cake
Before which snow settles on a frozen lake.
In spring when the snow has vanished
I'll lift the rusted cover on my well
And lean over to breathe in the water's smell.
It'll be pure. It'll smell of nothing.

Killing a Sheep

The evening meal was tethered
In the back of a pick-up truck.
Its black fleece didn't seem to fit,
Parted along the spine and hanging
Like an obvious toupée.
When we jolted to the lake
Its bleating lengthened to the wail
Made by a neglected child.

Bedu girls crouched beside the water
As my students stripped to pantaloons
And clambered to the scummy fall.
Then slipping, teetering, they dived
Their cotton underwear billowing
Like windsocks. The girls held up their veils
And ululated in applause.
The trussed sheep lay soundlessly.

'You are our teacher,' they said,
'The oldest one,' handing me a knife.
I felt its edge with a fingertip
But drew no blood. 'Take your shoes off
And roll your trousers above your knees.'
Three gripped the squirming animal.
I put the point against its throat, pushed.
My feet were drenched with blood and piss.

Piously they hung the carcase
From the pick-up so the blood could drain
While they unloaded brushwood
And gathered stones for a barbecue,
Which they lit with kerosene.
I paddled in the lake to wash the muck off.
The girls pulled on more veils
And averted eyes as mild as ewes'.

That night I picked through meat wondering
How I could have slaughtered with such lack
Of nausea. It was as if I'd gained
An iron mean of unconcern.
Later, while my students smoked or snoozed,
I sat fearful of scorpions
Yet amazed by clouds of stars
Above shadows of dogs among the bones.

The Barbarian Invasions

However much the last consuls longed
They never belonged
To the Longobards
Or their king, who made his wife retell
Her vows by drinking for a spell
From her father's skull.
Oh Commundo!
Oh Rosamunda!

Which brings us by a long stretch of pillage
To a more indefinite age
Of rip-roaring arbitrage,
Nifty little consultants laying about
Before selling up and out.
Call me a ticket tout!
Call me a commerce commando!
Lovely knockers Rosamunda!

Yet they still come in from the wilderness
To find a yellowing marchioness
On her knees in a state of undress
Reviving a wrinkled retainer.
Was it for this they drove herds of reindeer
In search of wonder?
Oh dejected shamans
Unconsoled by Mammon!

However much the barbarians long
To rewind their spool of travel they'll always belong
Now to those of us strong
In the easy arts of creating appetite,
Of confusing right with shite,
Of convincing them that their might
Lacks style. That shell suit!
That taste for beetroot!

So let us embrace these magenta-handed gentry,
Despite their dearth of pleasantry,
Their rough-shod entry,
And croon or con them into a rare side of life
Serener and keener than, say, the grief
Of a much-wronged wife.
Oh Commundo!
Oh Rosamunda!

Sawston Hall

This Catholic Tudor manor
Has been made into a language school.
Samplers embroidered with pieties yellowing
On the panelled walls, copies of portraits
Are all that's left of family history.

The new owner is Levantine,
Academic. He leans across at lunch
To whisper of circumcision,
'Not too early, not too late; inflicted
Between innocence and understanding.'

Outside students practise in the sun
Intent upon English for business,
Engineering, even literature.
They sit among members of a painting club,
Old ladies perched above sketches.

I inspect soft paper hardly touched.
Twelve strokes of maroon, severe as blades,
Have formed two water lily flowers.
I am impertinent, 'It is Japanese.'
The artist looks at me, 'It wants more life.'

Beyond her is a pathway to the spring
Where once coiffed daughters of the house
Giggled and dipped their handkerchiefs through scum
To blot their skin with holy tincture
Against spots. Now Buddhist and Muslim girls

Kneel to regard their own flawed complexions.
They pass the bursar poised with secateurs
In the undergrowth he's fussily labelled.
He mutters Latin names and observes
'They are the last of their kind in England.'

I think of the death of languages
As the watercolourist circles her blooms
With a blue wash meant for water.
Lily pads float upon this medium
And on them squat outlines of large green frogs.

The Perfect Haircut

Now that my double-crown has become a crop circle,
Left by aliens or, at least, unwanted genes,
I have begun to consider the perfect haircut;
Something I do at night, not during the day.
For in sunlight pink shows through the grey.

No longer do girls or, as they used to, boys, ask
'Do you perm it yourself or go to Sassoon's?'
I was Jimi Hendrix or Marc Bolan from the nose back.
Now when someone runs her hand through my hair
I take her fingertips and place them elsewhere.

My first haircuts were from those whose training
Was on naval ratings or in the Western desert.
Their instruments were blunt scissors and cut-throat razors.
They were the last apostles of bad breath and bay rum.
Then came my years of no haircuts and a wooden comb.

It wasn't till my late twenties and a steady job
That I had a decent haircut, perhaps the best;
A shop in Camden, the hairdresser Malaysian.
I learnt that she was living in the next street.
Her touch strayed below my hairline. We arranged to meet.

Just the one night and then mediocre shearing
For the next twenty years till my second best head
From someone very like her in the basement at Austin Reed's.
By then my widow's peak had lost most of its point
And such thin hair that she didn't cut so much as anoint.

The thickest hair can vanish like talent of a sort.
If moderately lucky, your true virtue is revealed.
If not, you design and wear a T-shirt declaring,
In front 'This ain't shaved. I'm just a real male',
And behind 'What do you find under a pony tail?'

Those who keep their hair change to a wintry glaze
Or else hide themselves with an untruth from a bottle.
Their truer lines are written beneath their eyes.
Better to age round and smooth as a stone
Or show how we all become, blank as bone.

My third best haircut happened in a Mumbai shop.
I sat down, closed my eyes, opening them at a rough touch;
Half-fingered hands, black weals on his cheeks, a leper's nose.
It's odd how even hair can respond to fear.
What I've got left combed out straight, without dandruff, for a year.

Stopover in Washington

I have gazed at the perfectly white grin
Of Greenland on the down curve of the horizon

And the long hearts beneath coastal waters,
Turquoise shapes beating against North America,

A state of mind, which has never grown a skin
To keep the humours of its substance in.

Its colours leak so my dreams take on a tint
And the ways I wish to love acquire a taint.

I stay in a house where I wonder what to do
Having been invited to be myself until I go.

Outside squirrels crackle through dry ivy on the wall,
Brusquely like shoppers intent on bargains in the mall

And a bird with a crest of flame clatters,
'What shall, what shall, what shall, what shall-la-la-la-lah.'

At the junction of an east–west avenue,
Prancing, but not rearing up, decorum being due

In the capital, is a black marble statue
Of a horsed general whose wide-eyed gaze reviews

Sunrise and sunset when light causes him to glitter.
At high noon he is more negative than anti-matter.

I'll fly south into the histology books
Where the cells of the body politic look

Like the swamps of Florida, brown protoplasm
Criss-crossed by darting specks, which leave short streaks of foam.

Between the swamps towers rise, beyond them the pulsing sea
And a life-size airport where my friends will meet me.

Canto for a Romantic Novelist

i.m. Gavin Ewart (1916–1995)

We Write the Last Chapter First

So handsome Doctor Sigman Tredegar
Does not really care for the lovely Lorissa,
But hankers after faithful Edwardina,
Night Sister to the bedpans and ailing infants
Of the National Health, having refused
A well-paid post in a Middle Eastern clinic
For reasons of conscience and perhaps for Sigman.

We Meet the Norton Commander

Your names are more or less unbelievable
As the English language is now becoming
Once upon a time there was a computer,
Which made up stories just as you do.
The grammar and syntax were impeccable
As only a binomial system file can make them.
But there wasn't a sentence anyone would have cause to say,
Lorissa pressed Sigman succulently against the reredos.

Places Generals Patton and Montgomery Never Reached

You're part of what goes in and out of the eye
Over the Oder-Neisse line as far as the Urals.
You've been translated and printed in different scripts;
Cyrillic, Greek, Turkish and Georgian.
Soon you'll be written from right to left or down the page,
More initial positions of the typeface
Than Edwardina's simple missionary surrender,
Which brings Sigman back to his senses.

And when Sigman confirms the worst fears of Edwardina's aunt
And says in that off-hand way of his,
Miles from anywhere in the middle of the night,
The car has broken down, darling,
This'll be rendered in Papua, New Guinea as
Ka bilong me baggerap, darling.

Lorissa's Oriental Wiles

You've made it eastwards along with the German
Hard-porn industry, holistic medicine and Walt Disney.
I can pick you up on a bookstall
Among *Dirty Girl*, *Herbal Medicine* and *Duck Tales*,
Among sodomy, quackery and quackery.
It's a pity you can't go back in time
And appear in hieroglyphs, which can read
From left to right, from right to left, downwards, upwards:
Lovely Lorissa pouted.
Sigman could be such a tease.
She had thought it would be so nice
If Sigman came down to the carp pool
And watched her bathe in her new linen.
Why did he have to go to that silly embalming
And draw out the vizier's brains through his nose?
Couldn't he leave them until tomorrow?

Cathay or Camay?

Why do we write as we do? Is it simply
So that 85 per cent of us will not smudge
What we've written? You, I know, have a perfect
Dorothy Richardson hand and have never smudged
Or hardly crossed out a word, just like Shakespeare.
Sigman pressed, crushed, *ah yes! gathered* Edwardina to him.

Why can't we write down
                          words in English like Chinese?
As if enlightenment descended from the heavens,

Understanding floating down like blossom or leaves,
Summer a glossy tree of ignorance,
Knowledge a brief change of colour to what
I know you simply can't resist calling gold.
Edwardina came out to meet him as far as Cho-fu-Sa. (Rihaku)

Lorissa Reads a Sura

Why not write like Arabic from right to left
When the hand reveals holy law as it writes
Though moving to the side of impurity?

in tents	*dark-eyed*	*Lorissa*
constantly	*renewed*	
of God	*the gifts*	*will you not acknowledge*
in tents	*dark-eyed*	*Lorissa*
ever	*virgin*	

(Despite the suspicions of Edwardina.)

Room at the Top

But you go on, 10,000 words a week
Moving from left to right like the Angry Young Men
Whose novels you've always considered arty-farty
(Pardon your French). *Lorissa tilted her cigarette
And blew out a line of smoke. 'You're from Huddersfield?'*

It's not quantity that counts though, but the single word.
Love? *Edwardina tilted her shining face to his.*
Not love, but the notion of a word.
A spectre is haunting writers, not the shattered Sigman
After his near-fatal accident on the ski slopes of Cortina,
But the person who told us we could write.

The Norton Commander Intervenes

His spirit has become religious and his visitations
Always start with a muttered, *In the beginning was the Word*
And the Word was made flesh. What are the chances
Of a computer writing that? But it's possible
In number theory. And the Word was made Lorissa.

Sigman to the Rescue

Sigman placed his stethoscope against the luscious
Page of the missal and heard the faint murmur
Of the Word beating. Sigman placed his stethoscope
Against the plate of the ticking missile.
How little do romantic novelists know
About disarming an unexploded bomb.
But Sigman is the only man on the spot with instruments.
Doctors can cure anything, even the English language.

What we speak is a language of conquest,
French, Norse, Anglo-Saxon, Latin.
It goes back and back and back.
And Sigman examines cancers you never describe.
Edwardina changes dressings on sores you can never contemplate.
And Lorissa? Why is she so tearful with Sigman?
It is not remorse at her wicked ways.
It is not a final ploy to get him into her clutches.
He is a doctor. He is a doctor.
And this lump keeps on growing and growing,
A lump in the breast not in the throat.

A Live Tradition

Live each day as though it were your last,
Edwardina sings in church, Sigman beside her
Sharing her hymn book. They do not think of Lorissa
Or of an English which has only two tenses,
The Past and American. The rest, Creole,
Australian, URxford are models of the verb *power.*
There's no future in English. Ask any grammarian.

Sigman is American, blonde-haired, blue-eyed,
A determined chin, shoulders like a football player.
He's in England to avoid misunderstandings
About income tax and medical insurance
(You are nothing if not contemporary).
Edwardina is an English rose, not quite as blonde as Sigman.
Lorissa is of uncertain, but English-speaking nationality,
Quite probably British, but not an English rose.

Indian Lovesong

Word follows word, in your case 10,000 a week,
And we create time. Lorissa and Sigman did this or that,
(At least in Edwardina's imagination.)
Wouldn't it be better to have a language like Hopi
With no syntax or grammar for time?

> *Sigman mixing medicine*
> *Edwardina pounding maize*
> *Lorissa adorning*
> *All kissing each other*

But there's no way to tell who kisses who first.
They could be kissing each other at the same time.

> *Edwardina's shining cheeks*
> *Lorissa's dark eyes*
> *Sigman's determined eyes*
> *All have the same lips*
> *A mouth kissing itself*

We Look Up at the Heavens

But for us who write in English word still follows word
And we might be losing a little of ourselves
Each time we utter and we never notice.
We dissolve, our texture thins, we become transparent.
Edwardina finally sees through Sigman.
Language, Lorissa whispers, *is a form of dying*.
There's no cure for it.
Our identities drift away like stars
As the universe expands and will not return.
Sound separates from sound:

Sig	–	ris	–	di	–	
	Lo	–	sa	–	na	
		Ed	–	war	–	man

We Look Out to Sea

Language flows from us until we die
When other tongues lap over us, waves
In an ocean with no limit we can discern.
This has happened before. This will happen again
As Sigman examines the voluptuous chapters
Of the Book of Revelations with a body scanner
And sees not the virus of Lorissa,
But Edwardina as the many-breasted Scarlet Woman.
The shock kills him.

We Look Elsewhere

I do not know what the computer would do now.
You, of course might never get to a point like this.
But I'd leave Edwardina and Lorissa
Dry-eyed over the corpse of Sigman.
I need someone to take care of me, one of them says.
We should go away together to somewhere quiet, says the other.
You wouldn't end it like this, would you Gavin? Would you?

Ode from a Nightingale

How sweetly down the void they float!
'The Nightingale', Mark Akenside

that music it's claimed I make,
not my style for I'm not a murmurer,
rather all at once abruptly burbling
from tall clumps of nettles, hazel bushes
as when you, blind drunk, settle on the wet grass
at midnight to hear me out and your students
carry you inside to sleep it off
and you clamber out of a window
to hear me again (I have not stopped)
and they bear you aloft on their shoulders cheering,
then detail the Polish lector to distract you
anyway she chooses as she does
most memorably that night
(do you, do you, do you wake or sleep?)
and the following day when you rise
clear-headed (it was good booze),
though somewhat fatigued, and lounge in the sun
while sweet slim Malinowska
of the lovely, lingering, lilting vowels
pops cherries and her tongue between
your most unmusical lips,
nor am I a true original
(every great artist has his sources)
as witnessed in the Middle East
where they've named Bulbul the Robber
after me, something you recall in Belgrade
when you pass an Arab embassy
on your way to a diplomatic do
where all is chatter and no sweet birds sing
especially a plagiarist,
as my rival the blackbird will assert,
though what can you expect from a minor artist
with his so-so so limited bag of tricks,
bawled from tree tops, while I hide

and am content to be unmysterious
not an omen, symbol or disguised immortal
just going normally through my routine
regardless of what humankind imposes,
something you discover in a forest
by the Polish border years after
the melisma of lovely Malinowska,
when you follow me into peril
off the beaten track through thorn and thicket,
stumbling into ravines and over
fallen beech trunks while I sing and sing
until you stagger out into sunlight
at the exact spot where you began
finding just silence, the barest breeze
ruffling the meadow grass, yes, finding
that fled is

To Billie Holiday

The age of innocence
Cleaned the doorstep of the cathouse
As the sound of happiness
Leant from an upstairs window
And called to her mother's son-in-law
To fetch her a fifth of rye.
There were long shadows in the street
But they were the consequence of light
Whose beams shimmied on the sidewalks
Leisurely and swiftly as Swing.
What went wrong? Nothing more
Than days staining towards nightfall
And the final dark when a voice
Grows hoarse with usage and bad luck,
Yet never losing a sense of time,
Immaculate conceptions of phrase.
The birds with feathers of blue
Chased you in and out of cell and ward
Until only tired old blood rose
From the roots of the needles of song
And even then, Billie,
No one could arrest your voice.

Nuages

You retire to lie half awake in misery.
I am governed by your climate,
What you say the world is coming to,
Clouds that lift with greatest difficulty.

What has this to do with Django
Playing in the margins of your distress
Trills and syncopation and the harmonics of 'Nuages',
Wisps of moisture under blues which seem limitless?

In your discomfort it's all a racket,
The noise of deals done behind closed doors
From the TV repair man's reckoning to a senate
Throwing out a bill to curb carbon-based emissions.

And Django's genius is a gypsy trick
Despite the way your breasts rise and fall
When you listen when you're better,
When your clouds thin out and scatter.

For the End of Time

i.m. Olivier Messiaen (1908–1992)

What must it be like?
What mist is seen on the lake?
Where most do you look?

Not to fold away into oneself
like a grasshopper hibernating
in a winter that will never end.

Even in the coldest times you must perch
the slimmest trace of green on your open hand
so it can make a joyful noise.

How must you live?

Aside from servility or commandment;
your work, your speech, an aside from them,
the footnote that outlives the text

with the unlikely, unlooked for, unlost
clarinet, violin, cello with three strings,
piano with many keys stuck.

Though suddenly to be released
and find the landscape stripped, all mud and shit,
as with Primo Levi,

is an afterlife that is insupportable
however swaddled with warmth, clean linen,
the music of the elements.

How long will the spring last?
How much has been lost?
Who are required least?

Not to be a name on a list
and thus be able to sing loudest
with the early willow tit,

its single note,
the blackbird on the roof ridge's high point
singing the great footnotes

that pass unrecorded,
perhaps elsewhere altering lives,
here, here, unregarded.

> *What must it not be like?*
> *What mist is not seen on the lake?*
> *Where most do you not look?*

Three Sighs at the Guan Pass

Suggested by the erhu of Yu Hong-mei

Something at the beginning of a century, which promises aridity in all senses of the word, to see a Painted Lady perch on your heel, its proboscis a miniature black straw sipping sweat from the tiny creases in your skin.

Elsewhere the dance of Whites, Dryad, Hermit and Heath Fritillary about each other like Yu Hong-mei's music and bee-like flies, scholars on the museum of a scrap of carpet. What could they possibly be consuming?

> Clouds thicken, darken then disperse,
> Unwelcome guests I keep away.
> Words quicken, pardon, then reverse
> Into the opposite of what I wished to say.

Don't tell me I'm being dreamt though I'm not clear-sighted, confused as I am with the ability to receive a thousand visions at once. My blood vessels fill, vesicles in my wings expand with air and I take off in a side-slipping quest for the source of the pheromone molecules you have cast yards, furlongs, miles off. Are wingbeats heartbeats?

> Shrouds glisten, darken, then much worse,
> Unwelcome ghosts I keep away.
> Words listen to each other then curse,
> Indeed the opposite of what I wished to say.

This is not for a friend as I am the one departing. Until I return a life underground, roots tangled together like fingers in distress, your heel on the earth above the buried, ripening Death's Head moth, not a shroud but a russet chrysalis eight inches down.

Elsewhere the Dryad drops its eggs on grass, on earth, on stone. Whose flight does not describe a brush stroke that never lifts from the silk?

> Herds quicken then stampede through the pass.
> Unwelcome gusts of snow bring worse to stay.
> Words from barbarians fill my glass,
> The opposite of what I wished to say.

A Scarlatti Sonata and the Golden Mean

For my mother

I like this one especially after
Its nervous trilling predecessor.
The piece's melancholy proceeds
Transforming the proportions of sound
Into so many identical rooms
Each with one woman whose children and griefs
Have never quite brought her to madness
Or away from the ideal of love.
I see her rise from an armchair and dance
Slowly, gracefully to the music.

A Middle-Aged Person's Guide to the Orchestra

Piccolo

Nowadays the mouthful of coffee you knock back
At a kiosk in the foreign city where you go to work,
Not the sound of a bird; siskin, goldcrest, treecreeper, wren,
coal tit, chaffinch, thrush, yikker of a sparrowhawk,
From the days before coffee was permitted to you,
When you could smell the oxygen from the roots of the lawn,
When rain was a scent of a trouble you had slept through
And birdsong soaked into you like colour from a child's book.

Rainmakers

Everything should become liquid
As the fellow guildsmen of the trumpeters,
The skin sounders, come into their own.

Camp followers of brassy, martial echoes
They should assert their power and render
Battles hopeless in driving rain.

For me nothing else can be called to mind
Except water as those half shells of copper
Covered in calfskin vibrate in monotone.

Haydn, despite a military symphony,
Set to soft, insistent repetitions
'God moved on the face of the waters.'

In summer insects dimple
The membrane of a pond. In winter
Footfall resonates on black ice

As breath pulses in plumes of water drops
And at any time a child's heels tom-tom
Within a mother before her waters break.

The first cry is miraculous
At one with the drum's noise of gravity,
Our sign that we are temporal.

For imagine hell as dry vacuum
In which we would drift forever
Away from intolerable brilliance

Begging Lazarus to stretch forth his hand
And cool our tongues with a fingertip.
In dreams of falling I do not fear

Bone fracture, but that endless tumbling.
The stick strikes the tense drum and I wake
Tearstained, in an ordinary light.

Fate Theme

My grandfather used to stop me in the hall
Whose panelling was mock-Jacobean.

He'd tell me he was the Chosen One
In a tone mournful as a bassoon's.

Perhaps a sombre-coloured voice like that
Informed the composer, who muttered to himself

'Ineluctable fate come and get me,'
Then drank a glass of water full of germs.

Such notions inhabit our ideas
Like large, untidy moths circling light.

We are too sad or squeamish to murder them
So open windows until they flap outside.

They always reappear next day at sunset
Stuck to windowpanes, showing their underparts.

Once my grandfather stopped me in the hall
And gave me half a tin of putty.

His death lightened and refreshed me
Like a house aired after a damp winter.

At my uncle's cottage near Stevenage
He'd gaze across fields to a stand of oaks

And the black corridors of space between them,
Which were round, bassoon mouths of complaint

At never having been wholly understood.
If he felt otherwise he did not say so.

Trombones

The sounds of mystery are widely spaced
In slow harmony on three trombones,
The simple noise that Monteverdi used
For descending to the Underworld.

Simple, but astonishing to Reason's lover
Who felt, 'If the lady wants it, why not!'
Until the stone commandant resurrected
From the smoky element of retribution.

Can Art still be made from fear of the unknown
Or from the notion of just punishment?
For now all sounds disintegrate
And not yield to a silent dread

Or even the natural sibilance,
Which is the innocence of animals.
A buzz contradiction drifts back
Like pestilence over the words we said.

And under the humus of Europe's beech woods
Rest long bones of history, which anyone
Can disinter to fashion instruments
'Beautiful in the pianissimo,

Loud without violence in the forte.'
They can drown the human orchestra,
But are 'seldom wanted' for enough of them
Accompany and fail to harmonise

With the jokes we make then disavow,
With our discontents, with our worry
That the divine survives, with our fractured,
Guilty speech, with the ghettoes we still keep.

A Violin Playing in Cairo

Between two apartment blocks
Somewhere above the space
Where a dozen cats live
And four dogs, each the colour of rust
Like the tins they sleep among,
A violin must be playing.

What else could the three old mothers
Dressed in black be listening to
As they sip tea across the street?
For once they aren't gossiping.
What else could the woman
In a red housecoat, which she fastens
Again and again as the breeze
Pulls it open, be dancing to?
There is no radio sound
Blaring from her balcony.

And what else could smarten up
The slack, untidy guardians
Of the military college
To something like efficiency
Since until now they've lounged and picked
Their fingernails with bayonet points?
No general's limousine
Slides through the barrack gates.

What could the violin mean?
Is the sound an insult
Like wealth wrung from this rundown city
Or is it a useless comfort
Like saying we are slaves
In the sight of God and must accept?

I do not know, but listen and listen
As the violin continues
Above and beneath clouds
White as shirt fronts in an orchestra
Until darkness settles
Like a burnoose over everything
Leaving only as accompaniment
The creak of tramcars on their rails,
The croak of taxi horns
And somewhere close by laughter
And the trilling cries of women
As a bride is brought home and to bed.

Postcard from Alexandria

Inside the harem you'll be tending
The eunuchs, Zanussi and Electrolux,
Who must roast meat and rotate linen
To their respective songs, 'Mmm' and 'Urrr'.

Then the pygmies will come in squalling
From the hairy billiard cloth.
You'll feed cleanse and swaddle them
Before extinguishing their ceiling fruit.
You'll turn to see how darkness makes their flesh
A liquid silence floating on bone.

Afterwards you'll illuminate
An electrical aquarium
And, with a tumbler of smoking fluid,
Settle to observe its sermon
On the horrible and domestic
While my postcard is abandoned
With a paper blini informing you
Of an award for writing oddly.

But here, Whump! the water heater shudders
From too much air and too little gas.
Wap! Wap! The ancient light bulbs shatter.
And on the wireless there's a love song's hubbub,
Abdelhalim's 'Ana laik alatool'.
He's long dead from a fire in his belly.

Friend, you advised me to seek the new.
But in squalor and a hostile strangeness
I've found only the oldest lines;
'Sound, the first thing made and from it fire and air,'
Lamented Hermes Trisgemistos.

So from my balcony I regard
The mute earth and air of the beach and sea.
Both are curved and shiny like bronze cymbals.
For between them waves twitch, froth then vanish
So the elements seem to meet and boom
Making what is above as below,
A white noise shimmering, shimmering...

Guitar

It's very wise to let go of intellect
As guitars change colour, the sun sinks
With the red wine's level in the bottle
And sea swell rises high enough to hide
The hulls of boats so only shapes of canvas drift
On water like geometrical clouds.

Give me a brick of dope, a do-not-disturb sign
And my pain can go on holiday.

It's also wise to let go of disappointment
As guitars turn black and the moonlight slides
Up the grape trellis like the torch beam
Of a lover looking for a balcony
Fearing he might not find the profile of his girl
Against the haphazard shadow of the vine.

Give me enough rope, a get-out-of-gaol card
And my brain can go on holiday.

But it's never wise to stay cold sober
As guitars revert to their polished brown
And sunrise imposes a proper light
On slack water where sails are loosely furled.
There the shadow of the insomniac stretches
As a straight line without thought or expectation.

Give me the trick of hope, the nod do-not-rock-the boat
For I'll always let the main chance go on holiday.

Exile

Here there is no hardship except the worst
Which is the absence of your voice.
We are separated by mountains
And a sea. I inhabit a place
Of rock, wind and a careful abundance
Where I cannot and do not wish to belong.
On windless days irrigation water
Rises over hectares where hours hang
Like slow smoke. On such days I am wakened
By the sound of a flute and turn to find
Emptiness where you should lie and dream.
I dress alone, in silence. By the window
The mimosa declines into blossom.
Orioles mourn in the olive groves.

Oboe

The creak of a washing line
Rubbing on the pole it's tied to
Or the keening of wind
Shifting paper down alleyways,
Air amplified in a coppice
As it is squeezed between branches
To a soft wail – pinched, nasal, plaintive,
The sound of pain suppressed
In domesticated England,
Relic of a grief,
Once massive as Siberia,
Made into a noise a man might hear
Within his head when he has lost his love,
Diminishing perhaps
To good manners, a graceful skirl
Over the surface of a stream
Or else escaping from the mesh
Of cultivated leaf and twig
To the bitterness of air round stone;
Grief unhampered, unappeased,

The ghost of love without object,
Without resting place.

L'Instrument Aquatique

'the overall quality somewhat massive...
the slack embouchure and broad bore allow of
considerable adjustments to the pitch...
thus a great flexibility for... nuance...
but also a certain lack of focus'

So let us don lime green spectacles
Before descending to a cellar bar
With tables on which we balance one glass each
And leaning tower of small change.
Here we might spot someone organising
Diving expeditions in concrete overshoes
Or selling futures in a process
For extracting gold from seawater.

There he blows! That Leviathan
Who has been made to play for our pastime
And 10 per cent of receipts at the door.
There he blows! That instrument of doubt
With which we make a certain hell for ourselves.
The notes eddy thought the smoky turbulence
Until nothing is solid any more.
The patrons are underwater creatures
And ideas of disorder slop about us
Coloured copper, turquoise and tangerine.

View of a Double Bass

It leans beside the stage.
The upper bouts beneath the neck
Are like the sloping back
Of a skilled labourer
Long out of proper work.
But it's much too empty and dark
For a bent self-sufficiency.

So maybe it slouches or sprawls,
A beast in repose or dead.
I think of the lion's side
In which Samson heard humming.
But a bow drawn on the bass
Never brought forth sweetness.
The glossy wood never ate meat.

Some oaks share its vacancy
When split by winter, lightning.
I can creep inside the opening
Of a willow hollowed by age.
But propped in gloom, man-made, useless,
This lacks a tree's gentle, ruthless
Inclination towards the sun.

The bass man is Brahms-and-Liszt.
The band will not strike up.
Indulgently images slip
From me and come to rest
On this shape of abandonment,
More human than I like to think,
More pick-up than instrument
Needing attention and a drink.

Harp

The lush blonde slims to inanition
So her notions of the way things are
Vibrate in space among steel wires and gilt wood.

She's so hungry that thoughts lose coherence
And become impressions shimmering
In hallucinatory slithers.

There might be sentences to be made out,
But when the individual notes are plucked
There seems to be no connection between them

As if someone translated word for word
From one language into another
Making original sense untrustworthy.

Somewhere unknown to man there must be women
Who handle structures of bone and gut to make
A savage, sensible music

Neither a food of love nor a diet of hate,
But thrilling passages of independence
Which play, play on until all sound stops.

Epitaph for a Piano

Let us dwell on the known life;
How, as in any biopic,
The conservative impresario
Was not impressed by her habit
Of shading loudness on single notes.

Nor let us recapitulate
How it took two others, one dying
Of cholera, the other deaf
To realise her unique gifts.
Nor will we be coy about love affairs
With various Central Europeans.

Nor will we draw a moral from the scandal
Of her decline when an American
Decked her private parts with screws,
Razor blades and pieces of paper
Then recorded the results on tape
And when he appeared on stage
And sat down at her with his hands folded
For thirty minutes doing nothing.

Rather let us indulge in gossip
Whispering that perhaps something
With so much ivory might have been
At least half-African especially
As she seemed happiest in ragtime
Or bending notes in the blues.

Let us think of her passing
As a dissolution into elements.
Brass and steel oxidise into ore.
Mahogany, walnut, rosewood
Become a forest where elephants stand up
And amble away, snorting, to a pool
Which gleams black and white as darkness falls.

It's better to imagine this
Than an oaf with a sledgehammer
Setting a world record for piano smashing
In four minutes thirty-seven seconds flat.

Obsolescence

Ophicleides, flugelhorn, tuba,
Euphonium, bombardon;
The sounds went deep to resonate
Beneath the human ear,
Leviathan himself sighing
When air took up the sea
As cloudshape and shook it landwards.

Ophicleides, flugelhorn, tuba,
Euphonium, bombardon;
The bass line of Silver bands
In valleys where the rain banged down
As prehistory was levered out
To be consumed in furnaces
For Britain's vanished industries.
Shipyards, engineering, steelworks;
They have dwindled to a vanishing point
So nothing with a noble and shapely line
Booms seawards through an estuary.

Ophicleides, flugelhorn, tuba,
Euphonium, bombardon;
No longer instruments,
But curiosities uncared for
So their notes are split and breathy
Like the voices of old men
Wheezing with emphysema.
If you whistled down a pit shaft
You'd call up neither featherweight
Nor slope-shouldered bowler
For the languid patronage
Of the sporting fancy,
But draughts of dampness, wicked gusts
Which smack the corrugated shed
Then tear away to provide
Undertones for the desperate
Whose last notes read, 'Coal Not Dole'.

Muzak

Under the civil codes of sound
The clarinet patrols at night.
The vixen's yelp, the barn owl's screech
Are silenced in the brief respite
From a sense of things going wrong.
Modest temperatures and showers
Endow those acres, which belong
To landlords thriving on good works.
Gusts, which twist like animals
Beneath hard heads of wheat, reveal
Healthiness not blight in stems
While in the towns merchants conceal
Windfall profits before they sleep.
Bumper harvests and little wars
Without a single loss will keep
A revolution off for years.
Each cultured citizen enjoys
A mixed band's jazz variations.
The ripe, asymmetric music falls
Among business conversations,
Casual amours and balance sheets.
No one hears that faint roar from where
Unthought of oceans must be hurled
Over the edges of the world.

A Viola Solo

I am always found wanting in a crisis.
I chuntered away to that feckless monarch,
Who indulged a silly wife and tinkered
With the works of locks until the revolution.
There was nothing in my nature to alert him
To a knowledge that it might not be enough
To be amiable and support reforms.

I do not belong with catastrophe;
Years before or maybe years after
When inflation is low and lawyers can be honest.
Between the violin preaching high ideals
And the cello bewailing immorality
And the decay of the state I'll temporise
Grumbling over promissory notes.

At such times people say I'm substantial
And impart richness to a score.
If the orchestra sounds bourgeois blame me.
I'm proud of it. Listen to the counterpoint
I provide to the suitor of a girl
From a different country and religion
As he waits in a damp, unheated flat.

His fashionable clothes accumulate grease spots,
His temper a ragged edge while her parents
Steadily refuse to countenance him
Hoping he'll go away. I remind him
His investments are sound, his prospects good
And that woodenness is not to be despised
When he notices that any concept of liberty

Now seems immobilised in the grain
Of the solid furniture. I tell him
Even temples in Greece derived their form
From timber structures put up for storage
Or the burial of a chief by a people
Whose needs were immediate and practical
Long before art or true love were thought of.

To a Cello Player

Once I feared I might marry a woman
Like a cello with broad hips and narrow breasts.
Her contralto voice would be exactly right
For long walks through the somber glitter
Of an English beech wood in autumn
Where we'd discuss the demise of culture
And, after two or three children, divorce
Finding ourselves too alike for comfort.

Now I know that love does not run true
To the black comedy of depression
And, listening to Jacqueline du Pré
Perform Elgar's Cello Concerto,
Understand once more that instruments remain
Instruments, that means never determine ends
And that even the most finished
Composition is never complete.

She plays a lament for losses in the war
To end all wars, maybe, but strips
The piece of imperial melancholy.
Such energy transforms this male tristesse
As the great horsehair bow slams the strings
And I am hurt by the knowledge
Of how the gentle must resist
With all courtesy, all tenderness firing.

Voluntary for the Massacre of the Innocents

From across the valley behind the hill
The trumpets sound quietly the way
Heinrich Schütz set Herod's need to kill
Against a consonance of subdued brass.

From across the valley behind the hill
The trumpets sound pleasantly the way
Old soldiers gloss a cruelty and spill
An anecdote as duty done with pride.

The trumpets sound heartbreakingly for Jill
Who dreamed of spring weddings and now must wait,
God knows how long, for Jimmy learning drill
Under a sergeant major's tarnished eye.

But neither Jill nor Jimmy ever will
Learn the meaning of their separation
However short it is. What music, shrill
And dissonant, can prick soldiers to confess

To sweethearts that they, unthinkingly,
Could slaughter infants or indeed that they
Could be untrue although, unblinkingly,
They'll recite the infidelities of friends?

So fetch a Christmas bottle and a corkscrew
Because Jimmy's gone to be a soldier.
Innocence is not knowing what you'll do,
Experience not telling what you've done.

And drink to Jimmy coming home to Jill.
He'll never say how misleadingly
The trumpets sound from behind the hill.
He'll listen, scratch his scars then sit still.

Fantasia for Horns

Somehow the unseen heralds
Of every final judge have come.
They lift coiled golden fossils
To their bearded lips and blow
So we will have to suffer
Not brimstone, but infinite regret.

Look! There float the shiny instruments,
Elevated by holy breath,
Glossy with light, crisp forms of stone
From which hurtle such gusts
As tear rook nests from oaks
And flatten acres of ripe wheat.

This landscape is ourselves.
In each of us hoof mark and footprint
Once met on early snow then vanished
As if beast and man had wings.
They were signs that the solid world
Had limits, that mystery required

Acknowledgement, that our needs
Should have been more than orderly
And should have risen above white lies.
Now it's far too late to seek
The undiscovered wood, which flourished
In impulse not deliberation.

We are left as careful couples,
Lovers of moderate passion,
Blue-eyed spouses managing
Within a brass-bound mean.
'Love me!' croaks the handsome liar
And has his pretty actions made plain.

For nothing can be revived.
All that remains within us
Is shadow on garden walls
Long after substance dies and falls
To leave a lethal silence glowing
Beneath huge clouds of unknowing.

To an Eleven-Year-Old Boy
Unable to Speak More Than Two Words

Awaking to the smell of varnished oak,
The waterproofed screws fixing the lid tight
So you must scrabble at the wood with your nails
Until earth sags through or your air gives out,
You would shriek, 'Door! Door!'

Watching an oak leaf turning an edge
And the flat surface towards you disclosing
And shutting out the spinney's insect whistle,
Watching wasps massed around a hole
Inside a blackberry patch drowsily
Climb the brambles then rise like flak
You would whisper, 'Door. Door.'

Seeing eyelids open after sleep
And mouths uttering for you mere noise
Which, for all you know, could be a curse
Or a song, you would reply, 'Door. Door.'

If you were shown the passages
In the pyramids closing up after
The sand counterweights flow out letting
The dressed blocks settle into place,
The widening decorated arches
Around the engraved wood of an entrance
To a cathedral where sinners take
Their naked worship and if you were shown
The unadorned steel shutters on the grills
In a prison you would observe, 'Door. Door.'

You could tell me what is behind me.
It has a frame and panels of pine,
A handle of brass and iron. It is
Painted white although unskilfully
Where the gloss has run and dried in streaks.
'Door,' you would say, 'Door. Door.'

Notes

The Clouds of Van Oort
This is the name given to the asteroids, comets and minor planets that lie at the outer edge of the Solar System. The Clouds extend out to as much as one light year's distance from the sun.

The Little Fiddler
The poems 'A Game', 'Invitation to a Pig-Killing', 'Fiddler with Card Players' and 'A Score Settled' borrow images from the poems of Ján Ondruš, although my poems do not even approach translations of originals. His poems are available in a collected edition, *Prehl'tanie vlasu* ('Swallowing a Hair'), published in 1996.

Two baroque composers for the violin are cited in the sequence, Heinrich Ignaz Franz von Biber (1644–1704) and Giuseppe Tartini (1692–1770).

Watching the Weather
'The Era of Consolidation' (or 'Era of Normalcy') was the name give by the ruling Communist Party in Czechoslovakia to the years following the Warsaw Pact invasion of Czechoslovakia on 21 August 1968.

The Barbarian Invasions
The story of Rosamunda and her father Commundo can be found in Thomas Hodgkins' history of the Western Roman Empire from which the title of the poem is taken.

A Middle-Aged Person's Guide to the Orchestra
For the smattering of technical vocabulary deployed in the sequence I am indebted to Robert Donington's *Music and its Instruments* (Methuen, 1982). There are three quotations from this book in the poems 'Trombones', 'L'Instrument Aquatique', and 'Oboe'.

In 'Trombones', besides the explicit reference to Monteverdi, there is also one to Mozart's *Don Giovanni*, where trombones are associated with the statue.

'Postcard from Alexandria': Abdelhalim Hafez (1929–77), singer and actor, sometimes known as the Brown Nightingale owing to the sweetness of his voice, was one of the four great Egyptian popular singers of the twentieth century. He contracted bilharzia as a child and this eventually caused his death. Four women are supposed to have committed suicide as a result of his death. 'Ana laik alatool' ('I love you straight/purely') is one the songs in which a 'Western' style was introduced to Egyptian popular music.

'L'Instrument Aquatique' was the expression Debussy used to describe the saxophone.

In 'Epitaph for a Piano' reference is made to a quoted opinion of Bach's as to the future of the piano.

'Voluntary for the Massacre of the Innocents': Heinrich Schütz (1585–1672), German Baroque composer. Reference is made to his Christmas Cantata. Another directly apposite piece for the origin of my poem would be the last part of *Symphoniae Sacrae*, a choral work composed in 1650 in response to the end of the Thirty Years War.